The Start of the
American Revolutionary War
Paul Revere Rides at Midnight

Allison Stark Draper

The Rosen Publishing Group's
PowerKids Press™
New York

For my father

Published in 2001 by The Rosen Publishing Group, Inc.
29 East 21st Street, New York, NY 10010

First Edition

Book Design: Michael de Guzman

Photo Credits: p. 4 © Culver Pictures Inc./SuperStock; p. 7 © A. K. G., Berlin/SuperStock, the artist of the engraving on page 7 was Paul Revere; p. 9 by Tim Hall; pp. 10, 11 © Archive Photos; pp. 12, 15, 16, 19, 20 © North Wind Picture Archives.

Draper, Allison Stark.
    The Start of the American Revolutionary War : Paul Revere rides at midnight / Allison Stark Draper.
        p. cm— (Headlines from history)
    Includes index.
    Summary: This book describes a series of events leading to the outbreak of the American Revolutionary War and explains how Paul Revere's warnings of British plans and British arrivals prepared the colonists for war.
    ISBN 0-8239-5672-5
    1. Revere, Paul, 1734–1818—Juvenile literature. 2. Massachusetts—History—Revolution, 1775-1783—Juvenile literature. [1. Revere, Paul, 1735-1818. 2. Massachusetts—History—Revolution, 1775-1783. 3. United States—History—Revolution, 1775-1783.] I. Title. II. Series.
2000
973.3—dc21   00-024765

Manufactured in the United States of America

CONTENTS

Paul Revere Joins the Struggle for American Independence

Paul Revere was born in Boston, Massachusetts, on January 1, 1735. His father was a **silversmith** and taught him how to make beautiful silver bowls and tea sets. Paul Revere became a silversmith, too.

4

While Paul Revere was growing up, Massachusetts was a British **colony**. Even though they lived in America, the people of Massachusetts were ruled by England. When he was 21, Paul Revere fought for the English **colonists** in a war against French colonists living in Canada. The French had attacked English colonies. This started the French and Indian War. The English won the war. Paul Revere was proud to have fought for his fellow colonists. He now felt more American than English. This made him start to think about **independence** from British rule.

Paul Revere fought for the English in the French and Indian War. The war got its name because Native Americans helped the French fight against the English.

First Steps Toward War

In 1765, Paul Revere joined a group called the Sons of Liberty. This group did not want America to be ruled by England. George III, the king of England, did not want to lose control over the American colonists. He sent soldiers to Boston to try to keep control. On March 5, 1770, English soldiers shot at a crowd of Americans, killing three men. The Americans called this the Boston **Massacre**. Paul Revere made an **engraving** of the Boston Massacre. He hung up prints of the engraving to show Americans how cruel the British were.

The British also **taxed** the Americans. One thing the British taxed was tea. In 1773, the Sons of Liberty sneaked onto a

6

Paul Revere's engraving of the Boston Massacre shows English soldiers firing at a crowd of American colonists.

British ship. They dumped 342 chests of tea overboard to protest the tea tax. This was called the Boston Tea Party.

7

Americans Attack British Fort

In December 1774, Paul Revere found out that two British warships were sailing from England. He guessed that the British were headed for a **fort** in a place called Portsmouth in the colony of New Hampshire. The British had a large supply of weapons at the fort and wanted to protect it.

On December 13, Paul Revere warned the Americans in Portsmouth about the warships. Several hundred men from Portsmouth attacked the British fort. They took down the British flag. They stole **muskets**, cannons, and **gunpowder**.

8

Paul Revere was wrong about where the British ships were headed. They were going to Boston, Massachusetts, not Portsmouth. By the time the British found out what Paul Revere had done, the New Hampshire fort was already torn down. The British began to think of Paul Revere as an enemy.

The American colonists attacked a British fort in Portsmouth, New Hampshire. They stole supplies and took down the British flag.

British Plan to Arrest American Patriots

On April 18, 1775, a British general named Thomas Gage gathered together 800 British soldiers. He ordered them to march to Concord, Massachusetts. General Gage wanted his soldiers to destroy the weapons the Americans had stored there. He also told them to find and arrest two men named John Hancock and Samuel Adams, who

10

were in Lexington, Massachusetts. Hancock and Adams were **patriots** who thought America should be free from British rule.

Another patriot, Doctor Joseph Warren, knew the British soldiers were gathering. He found out about the plan to arrest Hancock and Adams. Doctor Warren asked Paul Revere to ride from Boston to Lexington to warn the two men. He sent another messenger, William Dawes, by another route in case Paul Revere was stopped by the British.

John Hancock was a merchant who became one of the leaders of the fight for independence from British rule.

Samuel Adams was an American patriot who had played a big part in the Boston Tea Party.

British to Come to Boston by Sea

At 10:00 P.M. on April 18, 1775, Paul Revere left the home of Doctor Warren. Paul Revere knew the British would guard all of the

12

roads leading into Boston. He wanted to warn the Americans outside Boston that the British soldiers were coming. He sent an American to find out which way the British would be coming to Boston. Paul Revere told the man to shine one light from a church bell tower if the British were coming by land. The man was to shine two lamps if the British were coming by sea. Paul Revere was waiting for the signal. When he saw two lanterns, he knew the British were coming to Boston by sea. He got in a boat and rowed across the Charles River to warn the Americans.

Revere saw two lights shining from a church bell tower. He knew the British were coming to Boston by sea.

Paul Revere
Sounds the Alarm

Paul Revere was crossing the Charles River when he saw a British warship. He hid his boat in the shadows of a larger boat. He arrived safely at the dock. A friend met him with a horse. At 11:00 P.M. Paul Revere set off on the ride that would become part of American history.

Paul Revere saw two British soldiers on horses. He turned his horse around and began to **gallop** in the other direction. The soldiers hurried after him, but could not catch him. Paul Revere rode into Medford, Massachusetts, and woke a colonist who belonged to a group called the **minutemen**. Minutemen got

14

Minutemen were ready to go to battle with just a minute's notice.

their name because they promised to be ready to fight with just a minute's notice. The minuteman sounded an alarm to prepare the other minutemen for battle. Paul Revere rode from Medford to Lexington. He warned the Americans that the British soldiers were on their way.

British Plan to Steal American Weapons

At 12:00 A.M. on April 19, 1775, Paul Revere rode up to the house in Lexington, Massachusetts, where Hancock and Adams were staying. He woke them up and warned them that the British were going to

16

arrest them. Dawes, the other American messenger, arrived half an hour later.

The British did not need to send 800 soldiers to arrest just two men. Hancock and Adams realized that British general Gage and his men were after the weapons the Americans had stored at Concord, Massachusetts. Hancock and Adams rang a bell to wake up the 130 minutemen in Lexington. Paul Revere and William Dawes climbed back on their horses. They galloped west to warn the people of Concord that the British were coming.

Revere galloped toward Concord, Massachusetts, to warn the Americans that the British were coming.

17

Paul Revere Captured by British Soldiers

Galloping toward Concord, Paul Revere and William Dawes met a doctor named Samuel Prescott. Doctor Prescott joined the two men to help warn people that the British were on their way.

Paul Revere was spotted by two British soldiers. He spun his horse around and headed for the woods. Six more British soldiers rode up and surrounded Paul Revere. They took out their guns and forced him to get off his horse.

All through his ride, Paul Revere tried to avoid British soldiers. This picture shows him at the start of his ride.

18

Dawes escaped but got lost in the dark. Doctor Prescott went on to warn the people of Concord that the British would soon be there.

19

Paul Revere Warns British Soldiers

Paul Revere wanted to scare the British soldiers who had captured him. He surprised them by saying he knew about their plan to capture Hancock and Adams. Paul Revere told the soldiers that he had warned Americans all over the countryside that the British were about to attack. He told the soldiers their lives were in danger. He said that 500 Americans were in Lexington, Massachusetts, ready to fight. The British soldiers who had captured Paul Revere did not want to face 500 angry colonists. They let Paul Revere go. Then the soldiers escaped.

Paul Revere warned the British soldiers that there were 500 Americans waiting to fight them in Lexington.

20

21

Revolutionary War Begins at Lexington

At 4:30 A.M. on April 19, 1775, the British gathered on the grass in Lexington. Thanks to Paul Revere's warnings, the colonists were waiting. A shot was fired. People do not know which side fired it. That shot started what became known as the **Revolutionary War**.

Later that morning, British soldiers searched Concord for weapons they thought the Americans had stored away. The British accidentally set fire to the courthouse. The Americans saw the flames and thought that the British were trying to burn down the city. The minutemen opened fire on the British soldiers. They drove the soldiers out of Concord. The Americans had won the first battle of the Revolutionary War.

22

GLOSSARY

colonists (KAH-luh-nists) People who live in a colony.

colony (KAH-luh-nee) An area in a new country where a large group of people move who are still ruled by the leaders and laws of their old country.

engraving (en-GRAY-ving) A picture that is cut into wood, stone, metal, or glass plates for printing.

fort (FORT) A strong building or place that can be defended against an enemy.

gallop (GAH-lup) When a horse runs quickly.

gunpowder (GUN-pow-dur) A black powder that explodes in a gun and moves the bullet.

independence (in-dih-PEN-dints) Freedom from following others.

massacre (MAS-ah-ker) A fight in which many people are killed.

minutemen (MIN-et-men) Armed Americans who were ready to fight at a moment's notice.

muskets (MUS-kets) Guns with long barrels used for fighting.

patriots (PAY-tree-ots) People who are very loyal to their country.

Revolutionary War (reh-vuh-LOO-shuh-nayr-ee WOR) The war that American colonists fought from 1775 to 1783 to win independence from England.

silversmith (SIL-ver-smith) Someone who makes crafts and jewels out of silver.

taxed (TAKST) To have given money to the government to pay for public services.

INDEX

WEB SITES

To learn more about Paul Revere and the Revolutionary War check out these Web sites:

http://www.optonline.com/comptons/ceo/0428_A.html
http://library.advanced.org/10966/data/lexnton.shtml